Written by Dorine Barbey
Illustrated by Luc Favreau

Specialist Adviser:
*American Society of
Civil Engineers*

ISBN 0-944589-44-8
First U.S. Publication 1993 by
Young Discovery Library
217 Main St. • Ossining, NY 10562

YOUNG DISCOVERY LIBRARY

Giant Works:
Underground,
Over Water,
In the Air

YOUNG DISCOVERY LIBRARY

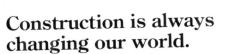

Construction is always changing our world.

If you go on vacation, your
town may look different
when you get back home.
A new road, bridge or
tunnel may be finished at last.
These are necessary signs of
progress. Things we need, to
go around or over obstacles,
like mountains or water.
They get us to school, work
or a friend's home, faster.

Modern construction methods
allow us to pass through
mountains and under water.
Today there are tunnels and
bridges over 20 miles long!

Machines help us to build
ever-taller skyscrapers in
a few months, instead of years.

Marble, sandstone and freestone

What do we build with?
With the same materials we have used for thousands of years. Bricks are made from clay baked in molds. Stone is cut from open mines, called **quarries**. A person who builds with stones or bricks is called a **mason**. To bond the materials he uses **cement** (made of clay and limestone) mixed with sand and water. The cement goes on wet and sticky but dries hard. In building, **plaster** is applied to walls before the paint.

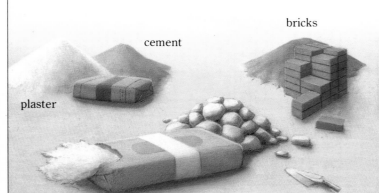

cement

bricks

plaster

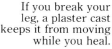
The Egyptians mixed clay and straw to make bricks. Then they baked them in the sun.

If you break your leg, a plaster cast keeps it from moving while you heal.

Steel and concrete have revolutionized architecture in the 20th Century.

These two materials have made great designs possible. Once it is poured into a form, it takes only a day for concrete to harden. Reinforcing it with steel rods makes it extra strong. Prestressed concrete has steel wires stretched inside. It supports active structures, like bridges.

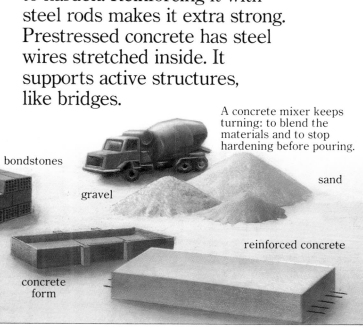

A concrete mixer keeps turning: to blend the materials and to stop hardening before pouring.

bondstones

gravel

sand

reinforced concrete

concrete form

dry cement
silo

bucket

power drill

crane

On the work site
Machines help the work crews
to remove rock and soil.

cement
plant

bulldozer

power shovel

dump truck

Roman roads were built in four layers, the top one of lava slabs. Soldiers built most of them.

McAdam's roads had three layers of different sized rocks. We still build macadam roads today.

Modern roadlaying is done by enormous machines.

From winding paths to paved roads.

Ancient roads were just dirt paths, following the easiest curves of the land. Once the wheel was invented, people needed hard roads that were wide and straight. Wagons, carts and whole armies could move faster. The Romans built the first system of paved roads.

John McAdam's invention

McAdam, an 18th century Scotsman, built the first modern roads. His plan had a hard-packed dirt base, then three layers of rock **gravel**, also packed tight. The road was also slightly rounded, to let rain water run off. Now we coat a macadam-type road with tar, and call it blacktop.

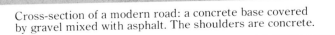

Cross-section of a modern road: a concrete base covered by gravel mixed with asphalt. The shoulders are concrete.

Heavy rollers "iron" out the roadway, making it hard and smooth.

Why do we need highways?
Because we have more and more cars. Highways provide faster and safer travel. That's because they have few cross streets, and dividers to separate traffic. Of course, you do miss a lot of sights.

A highway can go over rivers,
under hills, through mountains. It takes a lot of work to build one. Highways have **exits**, so you can get on and off. There are **junctions**, places where other roads meet. **Interchanges** switch you from one highway to another. All this has to be done safely and easily.

A "cloverleaf" interchange in Los Angeles with four levels.

A tunnel-borer, digging through the earth.

Tunnels take us under rivers,
seas, mountains; even cities!
And not only cars and trains:
water, gas and electrical lines
all travel through tunnels.
Those great builders,
the Romans, used
tunnels to carry
water supplies.

The tunnel under Mont
Blanc links France
and Italy.

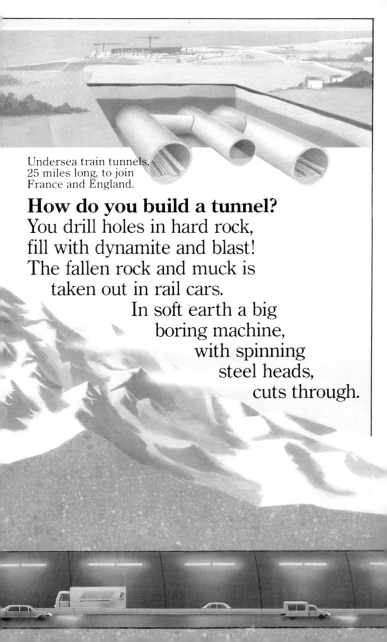

Undersea train tunnels,
25 miles long, to join
France and England.

How do you build a tunnel?
You drill holes in hard rock,
fill with dynamite and blast!
The fallen rock and muck is
taken out in rail cars.
In soft earth a big
boring machine,
with spinning
steel heads,
cuts through.

How do you cross a river?

Once people used rafts. Or
they placed large stones or
logs across a shallow spot.
Early bridges were simple
footbridges, made of planks,
vines and rope. The Romans
built wide, stone bridges.
Many of their arched bridges,
over 2,000 years-old, can
still be seen in Europe.
The semicircular arch uses
less material but is strong.

This graceful form was also
used for brick or stone
aqueducts, to carry water. The
arch is over 4,000 years old.

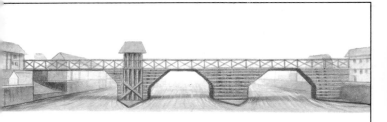

The **piers**, or supports, of this wooden bridge in India are made of logs. Under the logs there is a stone foundation.

The Concorde bridge in Paris is made of stone. Its arches have an oval shape. The first iron bridge was built in 1779 in England.

This railway suspension bridge over the Niagara river was built in 1855 by John Roebling. Later he designed the Brooklyn Bridge.

This wonderful bridge goes to the Isle of Ré, off the French coast. The roadway rests on 28 piers, anchored in rock under the sea.

Beam bridge

Arch bridge

Suspension bridge

Cantilever bridge

Modern bridges are lighter.
They are made of steel or
concrete—reinforced or
prestressed. Their foundations
are usually concrete, anchored
in underwater rock. Bridges
are built to resist strong
water currents and high winds.
There are four basic types.
A <u>beam</u> bridge rests on piers.
The <u>arch</u> bridge has a single
curve. A <u>suspension</u> bridge is
a roadway held up by steel
cables and two high towers.
A <u>cantilever</u> bridge is made of a
center span hung on projecting
forms on each side.

Dikes hold back water.

Dikes can change the course
of a river and stop flooding.
In the southern United States
they are often called *levees*.
In the Netherlands (Dutch
for Low Countries), dikes are
vital to keeping the sea from
covering much of the country.

The Dutch people also use dikes
to get new land from the sea.
One of the biggest dikes closed
off an inlet of the North Sea
called the Zuider Zee. The
dike is over 19 miles long
and took 13 years to build.
The area it protects was
drained for farms and homes.

The last part of a dike is being put in place.
Then a road will be built on top.

◀ The Corinth canal, in Greece, links the Aegean Sea to the Ionian Sea. It took 10 years to dig.

Canals are waterways, made by people instead of nature.

They give easier access from one body of water to another. Canals can bring water to dry places, for people or crops. A canal is easiest to build if the land is level. If the land is hilly, the canal will need one or more locks. The Panama Canal required giant locks.

A lock works this way: The boat enters and gates close tightly behind it.

More water is let into the lock. The water level rises and so does the boat.

When the water is high enough, the front gates are opened. The boat continues on its way.

Dams form great reservoirs.

They control the flow of rivers,
provide power for electricity
and water for irrigation. Many
cities and towns use reservoirs
to store drinking water.
Dams must be very well-made and
sturdy. They have to hold back
thousands of tons of water.
Some dams are made of earth or
stone. Others are made of
reinforced concrete, built in
a high, wide arch. The force
of the water spreads out, all
along the curve to the banks.

Look at the top picture. That's the way the
land looked before a dam was built.

An arch dam

On the construction site, a foreman and a worker discuss the next step.

How is a tower built?

Space is tight in big cities, so buildings go up instead of out. A tall building must resist strong winds or maybe an earthquake. A building can expand in heat and contract in cold. That causes **stress**. So, they are built of steel and concrete for strength. First, a foundation is dug. In soft ground, pilings are anchored deep into solid rock. Then it's up from there!

This metal girder is called an I-beam.

A reinforced concrete beam

Next, an enormous column of steel and concrete is erected. This supports the floors. Level by level, the building takes shape. Giant cranes lift materials to the top.

The core of a building is made of concrete.

This tower is covered by panels of glass and aluminum.

Dressed in glass and metal, the towers of Manhattan seem to touch the sky. Much of the concrete is well-hidden. Manhattan is a small island but a big center of culture and business. The only way to build is up—skyscrapers! A tower is like a small city. It has a huge heating and cooling system; generators for power, and a water supply. Fast, quiet elevators zip the people up and down. It takes about 3 minutes to get to the top of the highest towers.

Manhattan towers: the highest is the World Trade Center at 1,350 feet.

A great many people can live,
work (or do both) in a skyscraper.
The Empire State building, in the
heart of Manhattan, holds 20,000
people! It has 102 stories and
69 elevators.
Many towers have restaurants at
the top. Some have theaters,
tennis courts and even swimming
pools!
The tallest building in the
world is the Sears Tower in
Chicago—a mighty
1,460 feet.

An architect designs buildings.

From the first stone to the last drop of paint.

First, a builder has an idea and obtains the money. Then the **architect** draws up the plans. Before construction starts the town government must give its approval. The effect on the environment has to be safe. Is there insurance in case of an accident? If everything is OK the work can begin.

An **engineer** will handle technical things, like the structure of the building. With the architect and the job foremen he decides how the work will proceed. Many types of skilled workers are needed: excavators, masons, plumbers, carpenters, electricians and painters. Can you name more?

33

Can you answer these questions?

1. The world's highest structure
   (not building) measures:
   a) 1,821 feet
   b) 1,350 feet
   c) 1,914 feet

2. This canal connects the Atlantic
   and Pacific oceans:
   a) the Suez Canal
   b) the Panama Canal
   c) the St. Lawrence Seaway

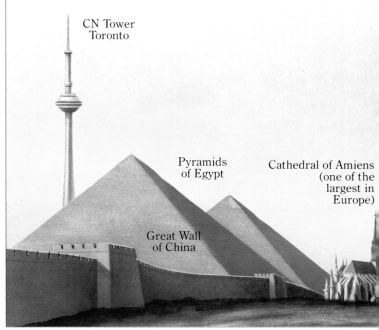

CN Tower
Toronto

Pyramids
of Egypt

Cathedral of Amiens
(one of the
largest in
Europe)

Great Wall
of China

3. About how long is the
   Great Wall of China?
   a) 600 miles
   b) 1,800 miles
   c) 3,000 miles

4. The longest suspension bridge
   in the United States is the:
   a) Verrazano-Narrows, New York bay
   b) Golden Gate, San Francisco bay
   c) Delaware Memorial, Del. river

Answers: 1-a It's the CN Tower in Toronto, in Canada.
2-b Ships using it avoid going around South America.
    The Suez canal links the Red Sea to the Mediterranean.
    The St. Lawrence Seaway is a series of canals, part of
    a route from the Atlantic Ocean to the Great Lakes.
3-b The wall's construction began in the 3rd Century BC.
4-a It measures 4,260 feet between its supports.

Sears Tower
Chicago

Hi-rise parking
in Chicago

Sydney Opera House
in Australia

Guy in the Sky

Gazing up at city sky,
I see a man where pigeons fly.
He seems relaxed, without a care
and no T-shirt. His chest is bare
in whipping winds. A one-man team,
locking steel bolts into a beam.

Strolling about on a skeleton floor,
alone inside of a building's core.
Beneath is a racket, a din, a clamor,
of chain, of bolt, of riveting hammer.
Ignoring it all, he puts on a show.
I gaze up in wonder, way down below.

Anne Proctor
(by permission)

Index